ADOPT-A-STREAM FOUNDATION

FIELD GUIDE

to the

PACIFIC
SALMON

Robert Steelquist

SASQUATCH BOOKS
Seattle, Washington

Printed in the United States of America

Cover design and illustration: Dugald Stermer
Text illustrations and maps: Sandra Noel
Composition: Scribe Typography

Library of Congress Cataloging in Publication Data

Steelquist, Robert.
    Field guide to the Pacific salmon : including salmon-watching sites in Alaska, British Columbia, Washington, Oregon, and Northern California / Robert Steelquist.
        p.   cm. — (Sasquatch field guide series)
    At head of title: Adopt-a-Stream Foundation.
    ISBN 0-912365-64-1 : $5.95
    1. Pacific salmon—Northwest, Pacific. 2. Pacific salmon—Alaska.
    I. Adopt-A-Stream Foundation. II. Title. III. Series.
    QL638.S2S79   1992   92-22962
    597'.55—dc20   CIP

Published by Sasquatch Books
1931 Second Avenue
Seattle, Washington 98101
(206) 441-5555

Other titles in the Sasquatch Field Guide series:

The Audubon Society
Field Guide to the Bald Eagle

The Oceanic Society
Field Guide to the Gray Whale

American Cetacean Society
Field Guide to the Orca

International Society of Cryptozoology
Field Guide to the Sasquatch

Great Bear Foundation
Field Guide to the Grizzly Bear

Contents

Acknowledgments

The purpose of *Field Guide to the Pacific Salmon* is to present, in a practical and accessible guidebook, basic life-history information about Pacific salmon. Most of the information contained here is the product of the research of hundreds of fisheries biologists over the last century. In particular, two major sources were of great help to the author: *Pacific Fishes of Canada*, by J. L. Hart, and a major recent book, *Pacific Salmon Life Histories*, edited by C. Groot and L. Margolis. For reasons of space, I have not made a separate attribution for each fact presented. I feel it necessary, however, to acknowledge my debt to J. L. Hart, C. Groot, and L. Margolis, and to the researchers whose work they synthesized. The reference section at the end of the book lists these and other works that will be of interest to naturalists and wild salmon advocates.

Thank you to Marnie McPhee, who researched the section on salmon observation sites. I recall with great pleasure seeing wild spawning coho the fall day our families were together (and our kids got soaking wet) on Eagle Creek.

I would also like to thank Bruce Brown, Jeff Cederholm, Jim Walton, and the late Glen Gallison for sharing their knowledge of and passion for wild fish and their habitat.

This book is dedicated to the restoration of a free-flowing Elwha River.

Introduction

Our eyes are transfixed on the water downstream. Surely it is them.

Strange wakes appear on the river's lightly rippled surface— impulses of water that move against the flow of current. The night's rain brought the river level up. This pulse signaled to the waiting salmon that it was time to enter from the sea. On the flood tide they entered and, as tide slackened and the river current quickened, they began their ascent.

They reach our pool three hours later—about 200 salmon. Around us they loll to the surface, rolling sideways. In the green depths of the pool beneath the logjam, they form a single body —that of a great fish that undulates in the current, its head upstream, its tapering body following. Beneath us they pass, spreading under the bank, on the edge of the current's thrust.

Along the North Pacific's shore, this scene is reenacted on many tides, on many rivers, each month between August and January, as various stocks of salmon conclude their tours of the ocean's great gyre by returning to the streams of their origin. The return marks one of nature's grandest spectacles, an event in a sequence of events around which the lives of the salmon, the humans, the bears and eagles that await them, even the forests revolve. Men and women mark their calendars, set their alarm clocks, and repair their nets or tune their outboard motors. Other predators time their migrations inshore to water's edge, their gathering to feed, and even the bearing of their offspring to this meter. For the forest, it means the return of nutrients that have drained off the land—nitrates and phosphates swept away in freshets, coming to rest on the continental shelf of the ocean, then stirred by currents and made alive again in plankton, small fish, and the salmon who carry them inland.

Pacific Rim peoples share a long tradition of watching rivers for the return of salmon. The First-Salmon Ceremony evolved among the cultures of salmon-eating people. At Celilo, the great falls on the Columbia River now submerged behind The Dalles Dam, native fishers awaited the first salmon with great anticipation. When it had been caught, fishing stopped until a ceremony was organized. The fishermen would take the fish to the shaman, who would cut it lengthwise and remove the backbone and head. It would be baked in a hole in the ground lined with choke-cherry leaves and covered with mats. Everyone would be invited to taste the fish; prayers would be said. Following the ceremony, fishing would resume, its success or failure determined by the respect shown the salmon during the ceremony. Thus, homage was paid to the returning ones, those who brought with them their fat flesh and its promise of sustenance, and along with it a sense that the world was working as it should.

Our age may seem too advanced for such reverence. On the other hand, we as a society still cherish (even require) salmon, and we still share this world with living things that deserve to play out their roles in the great evolutionary cycle in which salmon figure so prominently.

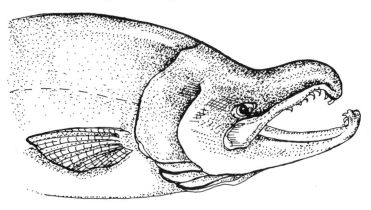

This book is a field guide to salmon of the northeastern Pacific, the region bordered by Alaska, British Columbia, Washington, Oregon, and California. Field guides to birds or whales aid primarily in the identification of species, with brief descriptions of behaviors observers are likely to see. Taking this approach to salmon poses certain problems, however. For one, even in prime salmon habitat, the fish are absent most of the time. And, given the diversity of salmon habitat along this vast reach of North America's coast, no guide could provide explicit, site-specific information that would cover that enormous range.

Instead, this book aims to help you *recognize* salmon habitat, those parts of coastal (and some interior) watersheds where salmon *will be* when they return to spawn or where, as fry or smolts, they will reside prior to their seaward migration. In the pages that follow, you will learn about the evolution of salmon and the kinds of salmon that inhabit the northeast Pacific. You will also learn about the salmon's behavior, about the gravest threats to its habitat, and about resources you can use to learn more about the fish.

My greatest hope is that this book will provide you with the basic clues to finding salmon habitat and that it will lead you to the nearest beaver pond, brush-lined creek, coastal river bar, secluded pool, or estuary in search of salmon—preferably again and again. Moreover, I hope your search eventually is rewarded with the unforgettable sight of the First Fish and its companions. If you are a fisher yourself, I urge you to praise your quarry and be mindful of the true meaning of its nourishment. And if you seek the salmon only to marvel at it, then likewise marvel at the forests, estuaries, streams, insects, and other living things that are part of the great salmon cycle.

Robert Steelquist

The Evolving Salmon

The classification and evolution of salmon have puzzled scientists for decades. The earliest descriptions of the fish came from Roman naturalists observing what we now call the Atlantic salmon, genus *Salmo*. European and Asian trouts (such as the brown trout) and chars (brook trout) were gradually added to the group. As North America was settled, Eastern trouts and salmon were recognized as close relatives of the European fish. Those of the Pacific Rim and intermountain West, however, were viewed as part of another group. The genus *Oncorhynchus* was first described in the 1860s on the basis of specimens collected from the Columbia River.

The problems of classification arise from the remarkable range of physical variation and survival strategies in fishes of the salmon family. Mature males and females of the same species can be strikingly different in appearance; spawning adults differ greatly from fish in the ocean; certain fish will remain close to their home streams rather than circle the North Pacific, returning earlier and thus smaller than others their age. At one point, ichthyologists (fish scientists) actually believed that what we now consider 5 of the Pacific salmon species were 50 species! Greater knowledge of the fish, along with advances in classification methods and evolutionary theory, gradually reduced that number.

Classification of Pacific salmon remains controversial even now. The current grouping, which places steelhead and cutthroat in the genus *Oncorhynchus*, was formally adopted by the American Fisheries Society in 1989. The accepted hypothesis on Pacific salmon evolution goes like this: The "ancestral salmon" was a freshwater fish, similar to freshwater members of today's genus *Salmo*. Early in the last million years, this form spread west across North America, then over the Bering land bridge and throughout eastern Asia by way of river systems, crossing the continental divides as watersheds changed due to glaciation and→

SALMON CLASSIFICATION

PHYLUM: ***Chordata***
SUBPHYLUM: ***Vertebrata*** (animals with developed backbones)
CLASS: ***Osteichthyes*** (bony fishes)
ORDER: ***Salmoniformes***
FAMILY: ***Salmonidae***
GENUS: ***Oncorhynchus*** ("on-ko-rink-us")

SPECIES:

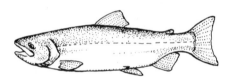

gorbuscha
("gor-boo-scha") pink, humpy

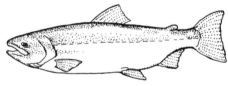

nerka
("ner-ka") sockeye, red, blueback, kokanee
(freshwater only)

keta
("kee-ta") chum, dog

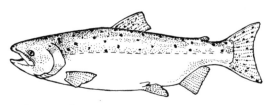

tshawytscha
("tau-wee-cha") king, chinook, tyee, blackmouth

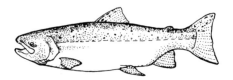

kisutch
("ki-sooch") coho, silver

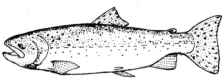

mykiss
("my-kiss") steelhead, resident rainbow trout (freshwater only)

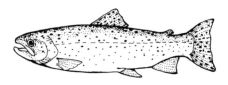

clarkii
("clark-ee-i") sea-run cutthroat trout, resident cutthroat trout

other processes. In the course of the ice ages, populations became separated by glacial advances and retreats and changes in sea level. As various stocks adapted to local conditions, differences in life history and physical characteristics became more pronounced.

Though debated by fisheries scientists, salmon are ranked according to evolutionary "advancement," ranging from those species that show the greatest similarity to the hypothetical "ancestral salmon" to those with the most pronounced evolutionary differences from the early fish.

The most primitive are the cutthroat and steelhead, which have forms that live entirely in fresh water, migrate only minimally, are voracious predators of smaller fish, and may spawn more than once. Next in the series are the two Asian species: *amago* and *masu* salmon. Both of these include anadromous (meaning they travel upriver from the sea to breed) and freshwater forms; neither migrate far in the ocean, and male fish of the freshwater forms may spawn more than once.

Coho and chinook represent the next steps. Coho have a long freshwater residence during which they are very competitive and feed extensively on aquatic insects, worms, crayfish, midges, and flies. Some stocks have been identified that remain close to the coast during their oceanic phase. Chinook vary in their freshwater residence patterns: some remain through their juvenile phase, others migrate to the ocean soon after emergence. Chinook that remain close to their home streams may attempt to spawn before they have fully matured—immature male salmon are called jacks. In Puget Sound, a major sport fishery has evolved around "winter blackmouths," a stock of chinook that appears never to leave the Sound.

According to the leading hypothesis, chum, sockeye, and pink salmon are more "advanced" species than the others because of

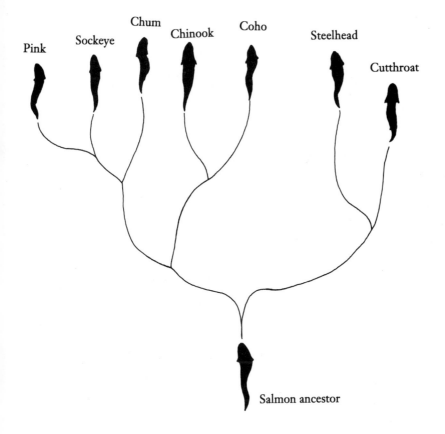

Salmon ancestor

their greater specialization for oceanic life. Chum salmon migrate to sea almost immediately after emergence and spawn in small coastal streams when they return. Sockeye have adapted strongly to lake environments (many stocks spawn not in streams but along lakeshores), show schooling behavior common among oceanic fishes, and graze on plankton. Pink salmon reside in fresh water only briefly, school extensively, and tend to spawn near the ocean. In addition, pinks have developed a very precise two-year life cycle, a sign of a high degree of specialization. Pink stocks in Washington spawn in odd years, while most in Alaska spawn in even years.

Whatever new knowledge is gained from genetics and other salmon evolution research, one thing is certain: salmon evolution has proceeded quickly and appears to be linked to the fishes' uncanny ability to adapt to very specific local conditions. Considering that learned behaviors are not passed from one generation to the next (young salmon never meet their parents), each salmon is endowed with a vast library of genetic information. This includes feeding behaviors, social behaviors, run timing, the ability to remember the scent of the home stream, orientation to currents, and other knowledge.

Perhaps the most important information coming from the study of salmon genetics is what we have learned about the role of habitat in salmon evolution. Each salmon species comprises hundreds of genetically distinctive stocks. Stocks vary river by river, and often within the same river (in terms of run timing). Habitat utilization by various stocks of various species appears to be finely tuned so that many kinds of habitats within a given stream are used by different fish at different times of the year. For salmon, the most effective evolutionary strategy allows each stock to use available habitat of a particular type, at a particular time. Overlap and competition are minimized and all of the habitats are used efficiently.

Human disruption of habitat has profoundly affected this arrangement. By destroying certain components of salmon habitat—straightening and diking river channels, for example—humans have displaced salmon whose evolution precisely attuned them to that habitat. Thus we have weakened those stocks, forcing them into less suitable habitat and requiring them to compete with other stocks and other species.

Our tampering with salmon genetics has had an even more direct impact. By selectively breeding fish with particularly "desirable" characteristics for hatchery propagation, we have severed the link between habitat and genes in many stocks. Coho, for example, bred and reared to attain larger size by the time of release, can swamp a stream system and displace the smaller (and more fit) wild coho. Interbreeding among hatchery and wild stocks has diluted wild stocks and reduced their survivability. The most tragic effect of such tampering can be seen in rivers where wild stocks have been purposely eliminated to make room for hatchery stocks. In the rush to meet the short-term demand for salmon meat in sport and commercial fisheries, we have impoverished both fish and habitat, the only real factors in long-term survival and true salmon productivity.

Hatcheries may play an important role in managing the watershed ecosystem for salmon productivity and for restoring endangered stocks. What has been missing, however, is a full appreciation of their impact on salmon genetics. Successful strategies must emphasize the long-term health of salmon stocks and their habitat over short-term economic gain from fat harvests of domesticated fish.

The evolution of the Pacific salmon shows us remarkable things about the fit between organisms and their environment. Salmon evolved in the cool waters of the temperate north and have distributed themselves for millennia in an environment of change. They have moved with the glaciers, been isolated by the falling sea and reunited as the sea again rose. They thrive in rivers that change from day to day, tide to tide, season to season, and year to year. Yet we humans have not only transformed the land, the rivers, and the estuaries that salmon evolved in; we have also transformed the fish themselves. Most serious, we have quickened the pace of change, brought up the tempo with which evolution itself must struggle to keep step.

Salmon Facts: General

SKIN, SCALES, AND COLORATION

Salmon scales are embedded in the skin and are covered by a thin epidermis, or outer skin. The epidermis is protected by a thick coating of mucus, which can be damaged easily by handling. Handle a live fish as little as possible and always with wet hands.

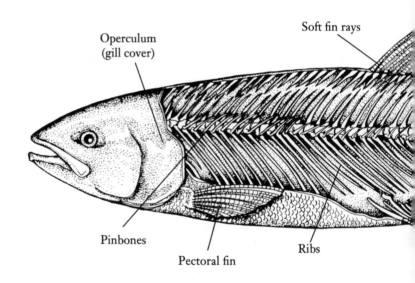

Soft fin rays

Operculum
(gill cover)

Pinbones

Pectoral fin

Ribs

Camouflage in salmon changes as the fish move from one environment to another. Fry have "parr marks," vertical bars that help them blend in with gravel. Once at sea, salmon develop "countershading," a kind of camouflage that helps them hide in the open ocean: from beneath, they appear very light in color, and from above they are dark.

Spawning colors help salmon find members of their own species at spawning time. The gaudy streaks on male chum salmon denote dominance.

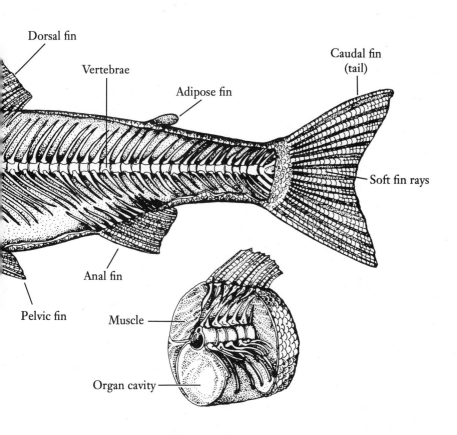

Dorsal fin

Vertebrae

Adipose fin

Caudal fin
(tail)

Soft fin rays

Anal fin

Pelvic fin

Muscle

Organ cavity

HEARING AND VISION

A salmon "hears" using two sets of sense organs. Lacking external ear openings, it has very sensitive inner ear organs that detect sound in combination with its swim bladder. It also has a line of pores running along each side of its body; this "lateral line" detects low frequencies close to the fish.

Most fish are nearsighted—they use other senses to detect food at a distance, and then move closer to visually identify it. Salmon may avoid areas of bright light because the pupils of their eyes are fairly large and don't change size the ways humans' do.

BONE STRUCTURE

Members of the salmon family are called "soft-rayed" because their fins are supported by branched, pliable rays, not bony spines.

MOVEMENT

Salmon can swim at an estimated 14 miles per hour (22.4 km/h). Tuna, by comparison, reach speeds of up to 50 miles per hour (80 km/h). Chums and chinook, although similar in size, have very different leaping abilities. Chinook can leap as high as 10 feet (3.1 m); chums have trouble topping 3 feet (about 1 m).

MAJOR PREDATORS

Juveniles: Arctic char, Dolly Varden, larger salmon, sculpins, and squawfish, as well as crows, mergansers, osprey, terns, gulls, and other seabirds.

Adults: Bears, eagles, gulls, harbor seal, humpback whale, northern fur seal, orca, Pacific halibut, Pacific whitesided dolphin.

Salmon Facts: Species by Species

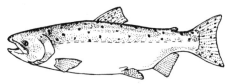

CHINOOK— *O. TSHAWYTSCHA*

Range: San Joaquin River, California, to Hokkaido, Japan; introduced to Chile, New Zealand, and the Great Lakes.

Abundance: Least abundant of the North American Pacific salmon.

Size: Largest body size of the Pacific salmon; length to 58 inches (147.3 cm), unofficial weight up to 135 pounds (61.2 kg).

Recognition: Greenish blue to bronze to black on back; large irregular spots on back, upper sides, and entire tail; body quite dark at spawning; black gums; conspicuous thickening at base of tail.

Freshwater/saltwater residence time: One form, identified as "stream-type," spends one or more years in fresh water, then two to four years (sometimes more) at sea, and returns to fresh water for several months before spawning. The second form, known as "ocean-type," migrates seaward within its first year, spends two to four years relatively close to the coast, and returns to fresh water a few days or weeks before spawning.

Spawning season: May to January, generally earlier for more northerly stocks.

Special habitat requirements: Chinook are most often found in large streams or rivers; many stocks spawn far inland. Because such river systems are often used for hydropower generation, spawning habitat has been lost on rivers including the Columbia and Sacramento. Spawning usually occurs in deep, fast water with cobble-size gravel.

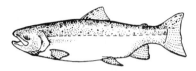

COHO — *O. KISUTCH*

Range: Sacramento River, California, to Point Hope, Alaska; patchy in Asia to the Sea of Japan; successfully introduced to the Great Lakes and Chile.

Abundance: Although coho are widespread, they are less abundant than sockeye, pink, and chum salmon. They represent less than 10 percent of the commercial Pacific salmon harvest.

Size: Length to 38 inches (96.5 cm); unofficial weight record of 31 pounds (14 kg). Normal weight of 6 to 12 pounds (2.7–5.4 kg).

Color: Blue back and silver flanks at sea, turning to dark green on back and bright red in fresh water; black spots on back and upper lobe of tail only; white gums.

Freshwater/saltwater residence time: Most coho spend one to two years in fresh water as solitary, opportunistic predators. They spend one to two years at sea.

Spawning season: Spawning migrations begin at sea usually as the fish have completed one full year in the ocean. Fish enter the rivers between August and December; spawning occurs between November and January. As with other salmon species, considerable variation occurs; northerly populations may migrate earlier, localized flow regimes may favor early or late migration for some stocks.

Special habitat requirements: Because of their long juvenile freshwater residence, coho require small headwater tributaries, where they compete with resident trout and juvenile steelhead. With winter flooding, coho juveniles use beaver ponds, side channels, and small tributaries to avoid the silt and currents of the freshet.

Habitat loss is due to streamside vegetation removal, filling of wetlands, and water-quality degradation in small streams.

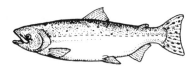

PINK — *O. GORBUSCHA*

Range: In Asia from North Korea to the Lena River on the East Siberian Sea; in North America from the Sacramento River to the Mackenzie River on the Beaufort Sea. Introduced to the Great Lakes, and rivers along the Black, Baltic, White, and Barents seas of northern Europe and northwestern Asia. Also introduced to Newfoundland and Chile.

Abundance: Most abundant of Pacific salmon, with total commercial harvest estimated at about 160 million between 1978 and 1981.

Size: Length to 30 inches (76.2 cm), weight between 3 and 5 pounds (1.4–2.3 kg).

Color: Blue on back and silvery on sides; large oval black spots on tail and back; spawning colors of red to green on back.

Freshwater/saltwater residence time: Pinks are known for their rigid two-year life cycle. They move quickly out of the river shortly after emergence and spend the first summer and winter relatively close to shore in the ocean. During their second summer their homeward migration begins.

Spawning season: Pinks return to the river between July and September.

Special habitat requirements: Generally, pinks spawn closer to the sea than other species; their life cycle involves the least dependence on freshwater environments of any of the Pacific salmon.

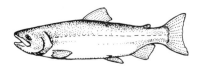

SOCKEYE — *O. NERKA*

Range: Sacramento River, California, to Hokkaido, Japan, with some populations along the Beaufort Sea, Chukchi Sea, Bering Straits, and the Sea of Okhotsk.

Abundance: Third in abundance after pink and chum salmon.

Size: Length to 33 inches (83.8 cm), weight to about 15 pounds (6.8 kg). Most adults weigh between 3½ and 8 pounds (1.6 and 3.6 kg).

Color: Greenish blue with fine black speckles on back; silver sides; spawning adults develop dull green heads and bright red bodies.

Freshwater/saltwater residence time: Variable. Some stocks, known as "kokanee," remain in fresh water throughout their lives. Most sockeye juveniles use lake areas for one to three years, followed by one to four years in the ocean. Timing is relatively constant within stocks.

Spawning season: Migrations begin in July, with spawning taking place from August to November.

Special habitat requirements: Sockeye differ from other Pacific salmon in their use of lake environments for spawning and juvenile rearing. Although most sockeye spawn in rivers and streams, some spawn in lakes, using beach or bottom areas where groundwater wells up through the gravel.

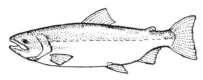

CHUM — *O. KETA*

Range: Broadest range of all the Pacific salmon. In Asia, from Kyushu, Japan, to the Lena River in Siberia; in North America, from the Mackenzie River to Monterey, California.

Abundance: Second in abundance to pink salmon.

Size: Length to 40 inches (101.6 cm), weight to about 33 pounds (14.9 kg); average adult weight is 9 pounds (4.1 kg).

Color: Distinctive blotchy purple, yellow, and pink streaks on sides during spawning; no spots on tail.

Freshwater/saltwater residence time: Chum typically migrate downstream immediately after emergence. Most North American chums spend three years at sea; many southerly stocks spend only two years at sea.

Spawning season: Chum return to their spawning streams between July and December, northerly stocks generally earlier. Some Puget Sound stocks spawn as late as March. In areas where coho or other salmon also spawn, chums often arrive and spawn earlier.

Special habitat requirements: Chum thrive in small coastal streams, where they spawn close to the salt water. Several Yukon River stocks spawn hundreds of miles inland.

STEELHEAD—*O. MYKISS*

Range: Southern California to the Bering Sea and the Aleutian Islands in Alaska. Introduced worldwide.

Abundance: Highly favored as sport fish, steelhead have been produced in hatcheries to meet demands. Wild, native stocks appear to be dwindling, and in many areas special fishing regulations have been imposed. Steelhead are taken commercially by Indian tribes and incidentally and illegally in the high-seas driftnet fishery.

Size: Length to 45 inches (114.3 cm), weight to 43 pounds (19.5 kg); average weight is 5 to 10 pounds (2.3–4.5 kg).

Color: Metallic blue on back, silver along sides; small spots on back and tail; males display a pink to red band along sides during spawning.

Freshwater/saltwater residence time: Steelhead spend one to four years in fresh water and one to four years at sea. Most common in Oregon and Washington is a two/two life history. As juveniles, they behave much like resident trout. At sea, steelhead are distributed widely over the North Pacific, as far west as 150 degrees west longitude. Because they can survive spawning, some spawn a second or third time.

Spawning season: "Summer run" steelhead enter the rivers from June through October, "winter run" between September and March. Spawning for both occurs between February and June.

Special habitat requirements: Good steelhead habitat is found in streams where water temperature remains cool and well oxygenated and where aquatic and terrestrial insects are abundant. Because young steelhead spend up to three years in fresh water, high-quality stream habitat is essential. Steelhead spawn at sites similar to those used by coho and chinook—some evidence suggests that competition for spawning habitat is minimized by spring spawning, after the salmon fry have emerged.

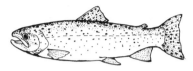

COASTAL CUTTHROAT—*O. CLARKII*

Range: Northern California to Prince William Sound, Alaska.

Abundance: Moderately abundant; however, the status of many stocks is unclear and the sport harvest of sea-run cutthroat is becoming increasingly restrictive to protect stocks.

Size: Length to 24 inches (61 cm); mature sea-runs weigh between 1 and 4 pounds (.5 and 1.8 kg).

Color: Blue-green on back and silver on sides; speckled with fine dark spots on back and tail; vivid red "slash" along lower jaw.

Freshwater/saltwater residence time: Coastal cutthroat spend one to four years in fresh water, and about one year in salt water. Like steelhead, they may survive the first spawning and migrate to salt water again. In one study, nearly one-third of the adults sampled spawned more than once.

Spawning season: As the local name "harvest trout" suggests, coastal cutthroat are common in streams during the fall. Their autumn entry into the rivers, however, is timed to accompany that of other salmon, in order to feed on dislodged eggs. Spawning occurs between December and May.

Special habitat requirements: Coastal cutthroat spawn and reside during their juvenile phase in the upper tributaries of coastal rivers. These habitats are vulnerable to logging, which causes silt-blocking of fine spawning gravel and loss of shade over the small streams. During their saltwater residence, cutthroat roam the edges of estuaries, preying on small schooling fishes.

Life in the Stream

STREAM DYNAMICS

Streams are complex environments subject to many physical, chemical, and biological influences.* All stream organisms—aquatic plants, insects, and fish—must constantly adapt to changing environmental conditions. In the coastal regions inhabited by salmon, streams are particularly dynamic. Much of the terrain is mountainous and streams can be steep. The climate of the coast is wet through much of the year, and streams rise quickly as water pours onto—and off—the land. Because salmon depend on streams during their most critical and vulnerable life stages, and because this environment is so volatile, whatever stability there is within the stream habitat is crucial to survival. Any disruption caused by human activity has a profound effect on salmon survival, which, under the best of conditions, is tenuous.

Three important factors influence streams as habitat for salmon: water quality, water quantity, and physical structure.

WATER QUALITY

Temperature: For salmon, water temperature is critical. Although they can survive within a range between 42°F and 77°F (5.6°C and 25°C), they are very sensitive to changes in water temperature. These are most often caused by removal of shade-producing shrubs and trees. Ideal temperature for most salmon is about 55°F (12.8°C). During summer months, deep pools are important as places of refuge when surface temperatures rise. Single logs, logjams, and undercut banks provide shade, and colder water naturally settles to the depths.

---

*Differences in meaning between the terms "river," "stream," "creek," and "brook" mostly reflect local usage rather than other, more precise characteristics. "Stream" as used here is generally synonymous with the others. I will occasionally use "rivers" to refer to large streams.

BIOLOGICAL AND HABITAT REQUIREMENTS IN SALMONIDS

	Spawning site	Time in gravel (eggs)	Emergence	Rearing site	Time in fresh water	Time in salt water	Return to fresh water
Chinook	main stem	*Fall*: 90–150 days *Spring*: 90–150 days	March–April	main stem	*Fall*: 60–120 days *Spring*: 1–2 years April, July–May	2–4 years	*Spring*: April *Summer*: July *Fall*: November
Coho	tributaries	80–150 days	April–May	Main-stem side channels, slack water	1–2 years (12–14 months) May–June	1–2 years	Late fall
Sockeye	lakeshore/ tributaries	90–150 days	April–May	lakes	1–3 years	1–4 years	Middle summer
Pink	main stem/ tributaries/ lower reaches	90–150 days (odd years only)	Late January, April–May	salt water	0	2 years	Early fall
Chum	main stem/ tributaries/ lower reaches	90–150 days	Late February, April–May	salt water	0	2–3 years	Early to late fall
Steelhead	tributaries and small rivers	50–150 days	June–July	tributaries	1–4 years	1–4 years	*Summer*: early summer, *Winter*: early winter
Cutthroat	tributaries and small rivers	90–150 days	June–July	tributaries	1–4 years	1 year	Fall and winter

Adapted from *Adopting a Stream: A Northwest Handbook*, by Steve Yates. (Seattle: Adopt-A-Stream Foundation, 1988)

Chemistry: The proper chemical balance is also crucial to survival in the dynamic stream environment. Salmon require highly oxygenated water, a condition that varies dramatically with flow rates, water temperature, and biological activity. They also prefer water neutral in pH, neither acidic nor basic. Dissolved solids such as calcium and magnesium have a direct impact on aquatic plants and animals. Calcium, for example, acts to make heavy metals less toxic to fish. Phosphates and nitrates affect the entire food chain; their abundance makes algae and other plant life bloom rapidly, setting off a chain of events harmful to salmon as decomposing organic material consumes valuable dissolved oxygen.

Salmon are so sensitive to toxic pollutants that young salmonids are used in standardized testing procedures to measure toxicity levels of hydrocarbons. Many salmon streams are particularly vulnerable to stormwater runoff that has collected petroleum and heavy metals from parking lots and highways.

Silt: Water is a powerful transporter of other materials. Rocks, sand, mud, silt, and debris are as much a part of the stream environment as water. Silt carried in the water can clog the gill membranes of fish, reducing their ability to extract oxygen from the water. Too much silt deposited over spawning gravel can deprive developing eggs of oxygen-rich water that normally percolates in the spaces between the pebbles.

WATER QUANTITY

The amount of water flowing in a salmon stream is also important. Too much water can overpower weak returning spawners and flush overwintering juveniles downstream. High flows can erode spawning beds, flushing eggs out of the gravel. Rolling boulders, stumps, and logs can gouge the bottom and banks of a stream, rearranging the habitat dramatically. Stream systems that flush heavily or frequently may accumulate fewer nutrients and develop fewer stable microhabitats than systems whose flows are less extreme. Numerous studies have shown that, following severe floods, insects and other aquatic organisms may be temporarily eliminated from a stream.

Too little water makes riffles impassable and isolates fish in pools where they are vulnerable to predators, lethal temperatures, and low oxygen content. Inadequate water flow is one of the major threats to salmon runs throughout much of their range. Water managed for irrigation and hydropower generation is often unavailable at precisely the time that salmon need it most. Hydroelectric dams, for example, reduce their flows when juveniles are traveling downstream. The young fish may pass through turbines or simply stop moving altogether as the water collects in dam reservoirs.

STRUCTURE

For salmon, the quality of stream habitat is closely related to its structure—the number and arrangement of pools, riffles and runs, side channels, and barriers.

Pools offer deep water, shade, the protective cover of boulders and submerged logs, and reduced current or turbulence. In pools, fish can find eddies and countercurrents that enable them to hold a position facing upstream while minimizing their energy expenditure. Thus, they can stay relatively quiet as drifting food comes to them or when they are conserving energy during the spawning run. Downed logs in stream ecosystems are crucial to the formation of pools and "stepped pools" as habitat. Studies have shown that the abundance of coho in forest streams is directly related to the presence and volume of pools. Pools created by logjams are capable of supporting hundreds of juvenile salmon. The loss of large standing trees along streams threatens the process by which pools of the future will be formed.

Riffles and runs are factories for aquatic insects and important sources of oxygen. Mayfly and stone fly nymphs, caddis fly worms in their cases, beetle larvae, and many other insect forms thrive in the rocks of the riffle. Boulder-strewn runs and cobble bottom create a three-dimensional mosaic of cover and allow more fish to inhabit the same reach. For coho, cutthroat, and steelhead juveniles, fish density is often determined by the number of feeding stations: the more boulders and the greater diversity in bottom textures, the more fish.

Side channels, meanders, and accessible overwintering ponds are crucial to juveniles as rich feeding habitat and as refuges during peak flooding. These are abandoned or partly abandoned stream courses that continue to carry water from hillside springs, percolation through the river bed, or periodic river overflows. Many contain ponds created or maintained by beavers. Along with small tributaries, all of these habitats play important roles at various times during the freshwater phase of the salmon's life. Their importance is often unrecognized, particularly in connection with timber harvesting activities.

Barriers have the most obvious structural impact on salmonid habitat in streams. On a grand scale, dams such as those on the Sacramento, Columbia, and Elwha rivers have eliminated sea-running fish from hundreds of miles of river habitat. On a much smaller scale, man-made structures such as poorly designed culverts also prevent fish from using otherwise useful habitat. Before managers fully understood the life histories of salmon, structures were designed only to allow passage of adult fish, and not young fry or fingerlings. Also, in some cases, barriers are created by actions that change the flow regime of the river. In 1913, rocks blasted in Hell's Gorge on the Fraser River during railroad construction so constricted the canyon that sockeye runs were unable to pass. Millions of fish died below the obstruction. In other cases, irrigation withdrawals can reduce stream flow to the point where fish have inadequate water in which to ascend the rapids to their spawning grounds.

Salmon evolution seems to favor stocks and species that spend the least amount of time in the freshwater environment. Yet all salmon species require the stream environment in order to reproduce. It is here that they are most vulnerable. Over the millennia, different conditions on thousands of streams and rivers have forged the genetic chains of survival. Here, salmon have been exposed to the major conditions that set their biological clocks and determine their fundamental biological and social makeup. We have learned the hard way that wild salmon survive only when the streams that nurture them survive.

Salmon Life Cycle

Death from
- predators
- disturbance of gravel
- pollution
- temperature changes

Death from
- predators
- pollution
- habitat destruction

EGGS IN GRAVEL

ALEVIN EMERGE FROM GRAVEL

COHO, STEELHEAD, CUTTHROAT, SOCKEYE, AND SOME CHINOOK LIVE IN FRESH WATER AS JUVENILES

CHUM, PINK, AND SOME CHINOOK MIGRATE DIRECTLY TO SALT WATER

SMOLTS ADAPT TO SALT WATER

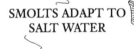

Death from
- predators
- habitat destruction
- delays in downstream migration

YOUNG ADULTS

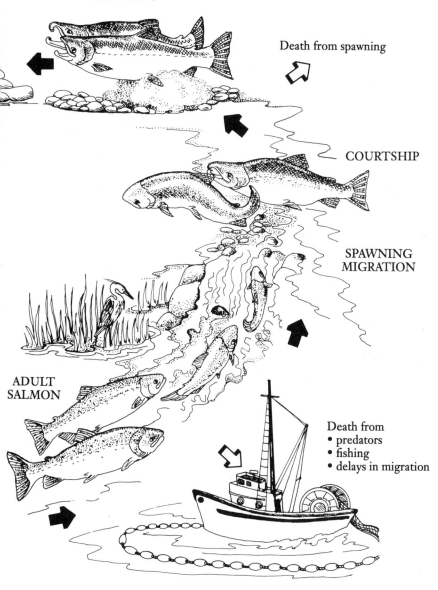

SPAWNING

Death from spawning

COURTSHIP

SPAWNING
MIGRATION

ADULT
SALMON

Death from
• predators
• fishing
• delays in migration

The Estuary and the Sea

Estuaries occur where coastal rivers enter the sea, creating a mix of fresh- and saltwater habitats. These habitats change with each tide. During the flood, ocean water pulses into the estuary and up the lower reaches of the river. At ebb, fresh water pours into the estuary basin, pushing a wedge of lighter fresh water and riverborne sediments into the estuary.

Protected inner waters of estuaries, laden with sediment, form the richest of coastal environments. Their productivity far exceeds that of either the finest agricultural land or the open ocean. The vast expanses of mudflat harbor thousands of invertebrates per cubic foot of material, which in turn support diverse higher forms, including salmon, mammals, and birds. Their importance to salmon comes from their structural complexity and their productivity. Estuary margins include eelgrass beds and salt marshes, habitats that hold nutrients and serve as nurseries for many tiny organisms, including invertebrates and fish larvae.

Our recognition of the ecological significance of estuaries arrived late; many of America's original estuaries have been lost to dredging and filling. Between 1958 and 1978 alone, 7 percent of the nation's estuaries were destroyed. Industrial pollution has also taken its toll. Early sawmills disposed of sawdust by filling estuary edges; pulp and paper mills dumped potent waste products directly into estuary waters. And the press of industrialization has led to the filling and "hardening" of estuary shores and the deepening of channels.

For salmon, the estuary represents a transition between the worlds of river and of sea. The passage outward involves the transformation from fresh water to salt water, a change with amazingly complex body-chemistry implications. The fish lose the markings that camouflage them against the stream's gravel and take on a silvery color. In salt water, salmon grow rapidly as they feed on plankton and small fish. Two-year-old coho, for example, leaving the stream at about 4 inches (10.2 cm) long may double in size in a matter of weeks.

Behavior changes too. Young salmon school in salt water. For chums, pinks, and sockeye, this schooling differs little from schooling behavior in the nursery stream or lake. For coho and chinook, however, schooling is an adaptation to saltwater life. Highly territorial and individualistic in streams, coho and chinook bunch up in the estuary, a habit that will improve their chance of survival in the open ocean.

COHO

By the time coho enter the estuary, they can be as old as two years. Once in salt water, they appear to remain fairly close to shore, feeding on marine invertebrates. As coho grow, their diet begins to include juvenile fish, including chum and pink salmon, smelt, and sand lance. Gradually, they wander farther and farther away from their home streams and estuaries—though they remain relatively close to the coast, where they avoid open-ocean predators.

CHINOOK

Chinook rely on coastal wetlands for juvenile habitat. Chinook migrate downstream at a young age and take up residence in coastal estuaries where salinity is low. Here, they gradually adapt to salt water by staying close to salt marsh edges during low tide and moving into river channels and sloughs at high tide. Growth is rapid during the chinook's estuary residence: over a period of about two months, the fish can triple in size. The length of stay in the estuary is thought to depend on how quickly they outgrow their prey—once they are large enough to eat small fish, they move away from shore.

SOCKEYE

Sockeye typically migrate into salt water during the spring and remain in the estuary for several months, feeding around tidal marshes and sloughs. Here, they often intermix with schools of pink and chum salmon. Movement offshore follows the growth of plankton in the summer months.

CHUM

Like chinook, chum salmon depend heavily on salt marsh and eelgrass beds as estuary habitat. When they are flooded by high tides, chum move through eelgrass meadows and salt marsh vegetation, feeding on small invertebrates. Gradually, as zooplankton populations increase farther offshore, the chum follow, with larger fish moving first.

PINK

Pink salmon typically migrate en masse out of their home stream shortly after emergence. Schools of tens of thousands of the tiny fry move through the shallow estuary margins, in water only a few inches deep. In Puget Sound, schools of pinks have been observed avoiding the deeper water of marinas and off bulkheads, where they are vulnerable to predators that require deeper water.

STEELHEAD

Steelhead enter the estuary after one or two years in fresh water. Like coho, which display solitary and predatory habits in the stream, steelhead become less territorial in salt water.

CUTTHROAT

Cutthroat remain closer to their native streams than any of the other species of Pacific salmon. For sea-run cutthroat, a one- or two-year stream residency is followed by one or more years in salt water. In the estuary, cutthroat grow rapidly, feeding opportunistically on estuary invertebrates and juvenile fishes. During summer months, small groups of cutthroats follow schools of sand lance and other prey species along beaches and into stream mouths and estuary inlets.

The Great Ocean Pasture

According to the most common theory of salmon evolution, these fish have followed a life cycle of going to sea in order to overcome the limits of food and space in freshwater habitats. In the northeast Pacific, ocean currents and climatic conditions combine to produce coastal upwelling, which draws nutrients from the ocean depths upward into the sunlit shallows of the continental shelf. Here, the alchemy of photosynthesis converts the sunlight and nutrients into food energy, first in the form of phytoplankton and then gradually up the whole food chain. Large schools of salmon of many stocks and several species comb the ocean. Prey varies as the salmon grow, with younger fish eating the larvae of crabs, barnacles, and other invertebrates. Gradually sand lance, herring, other salmon, rockfish, and squid become the food staples of ocean-phase salmon.

The general migratory pattern for salmon in the North Pacific has a broad, circular shape. As the fish enter the ocean, they move to the north and northwest. Sockeye, pink, and chum salmon move in large schools in a relatively narrow belt along the Northwest Coast, into the Gulf of Alaska, and out toward the Aleutian Islands. From there they move to the south and east. Chinook, coho, and steelhead appear to spread out, with some remaining relatively close to the coast, others moving more directly west, and still others following the coastline toward the north and northwest.

Life in the ocean favors larger fish and large schools. Size upon entry into the ocean seems to be an important factor in ocean survival for all species. For any given fish, avoiding predators becomes easier within a larger group. Salmon passing through the hunting grounds of fur seals in the Pribilof Islands enjoy the advantage of "swamping" the fur seal herd—the fish pass within reach of the seals in such numbers that even the voracious seal can only eat so many before the salmon are beyond its range.

The salmon's return to the estuary is also remarkable. For a fish to travel thousands of miles in the open ocean and then locate and return to the estuary of its birth river seems to defy all odds. Several theories have been proposed to account for the salmon's legendary homing instinct. An explanation currently given support by fisheries scientists holds that salmon navigate at sea with the aid of an inner magnetic map and a strong sense of day length. In this model, a given fish usually knows approximately where it is in relation to its home stream. As the advance of the season is signaled by changing day length, the fish moves more or less directly toward the river mouth. During the "final approach," the salmon's sense of smell comes into play, drawing it toward water smells encountered during the juvenile phases of life.

Once the salmon enters the estuary and begins the ascent of its home stream, its final physical transformation also begins. In a matter of weeks its firm, silvery mass of muscle softens; the fish darkens, takes on its spawning colors, and changes shape.

For most salmon species, inward migration through estuaries is as brief as possible. The fish explore estuary mouths, entering and testing for signs of the right river. During fall months, when rivers may be low, schools of inbound salmon often bunch up in the estuary or river mouth awaiting the first surges of fall runoff or high tides. Here, they can be seen leaping out of the water, a behavior not fully understood. They also may cruise close to the surface, their dorsal fins showing. The final passage back through the estuary of its natal river is only a prelude to a salmon's final acts: navigating upstream against current and time, spawning the next generation, and dying in the river that gave it life.

Reproduction and the Return to the Ancestral Gravel

THE SPAWNING RUN

The sight of a leaping salmon, struggling desperately against a torrent, is one of nature's most poignant symbols. It represents life as a cycle, the promise of return, the power of instincts, defiance of the odds of survival, and singleness of purpose. The way salmon spawn also sets them apart from most other organisms and gives us clues to the wonderful mechanics of evolution and adaptation.

Salmon are *anadromous* fish. This means that they spend part of their lives in fresh water, some in salt water, and then mate and produce offspring in fresh water. (Eels of the Atlantic Ocean are *catadromous*—they spend their lives in fresh and salt water but breed in the sea.) This strategy of using different habitats at different times of the fishes' lives has evolved in a way that lets the salmon overcome the food and space limits of the freshwater environment.

The second unique feature of salmon reproduction is mass spawning. Salmon of one stock spawn together. This has the effect of making individuals within a given stock genetically very similar because it reduces the chances that genes from other stocks will be introduced by crossbreeding. Mass spawning also makes this phase of the salmon's life a conspicuous event, a spectacle of nature that occurs in thousands of streams and rivers along the Pacific Coast.

OVER THE BAR

The spawning run begins far out at sea, when day length and magnetic cues trigger the urge to return within the fish. The journey home begins. The precision with which salmon are able

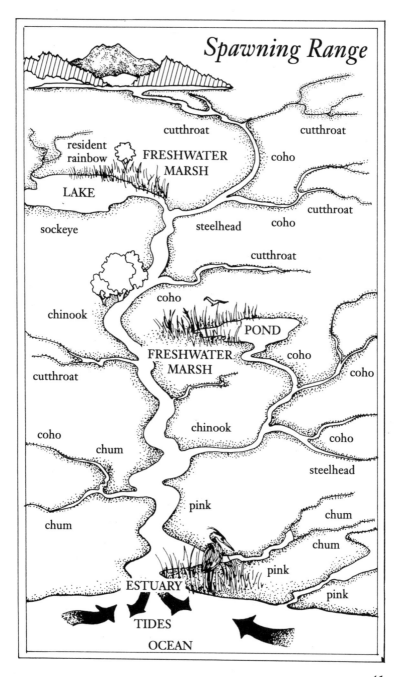

Spawning Range

cutthroat

cutthroat

resident
rainbow

FRESHWATER
MARSH

coho

LAKE

cutthroat

sockeye

steelhead

coho

coho

cutthroat

coho

chinook

POND

FRESHWATER
MARSH

coho

coho

cutthroat

chinook

coho

coho

chum

steelhead

chum

pink

chum

chum

chum

pink

ESTUARY

pink

pink

TIDES

OCEAN

to locate and reach their home stream puzzles many scientists. Although some straying occurs, most salmon surviving the ocean journey—even though separated from other salmon of their own stock—are able to find their own stream at about the same time as their cohorts. Salmon often "test" rivers other than their own, entering the estuary or lower river and then retreating to the sea and moving farther along the coast. And although salmon appear to show overwhelming loyalty to their home stream, a large-scale catastrophe within their river can force them to adopt another river en masse. The best example of this occurred following the 1980 eruption of Mount St. Helens. When the Toutle River salmon returned to the river, they found it choked with ash and silt, abandoned it, and spawned instead in the Kalama River.

After entering the river, fish move quickly upstream. On large rivers, this passage may be relatively continual. The salmon orient themselves against the current, finding that area within the river channel where current is noticeable but not strong enough to completely exhaust them. In large rivers with huge reservoirs behind dams, the salmon may temporarily lose the current when they enter the reservoir. Delayed by slack water, they lose precious time milling about in search of physical and chemical clues about the water's source.

On smaller rivers, where the river breaks into pools, riffles, and rapids, the salmon spread out into bunches. They may loiter in pools if the water is low, as it often is in late summer and fall. When conditions are right, groups will surge forward. Upon passing through quick water, the fish will gather again in the quiet, regain their strength, and continue upstream. They tend to move as long strands, hugging the deeper channels and shaded areas of the stream. Individuals and pairs can be seen in pools, streaking up and down as other fish remain quiet. At shallow riffles, where the river steps down a gravel ramp, running fish raise rooster tails of water as they speed over the rocks.

THE HOME GRAVEL

Once at their ancestral gravel, salmon mill about as the sac around the eggs loosens and the spawning urge quickens. Small, precocious males called jacks look for opportunities to challenge larger males for access to the females. Females search for suitable egg-laying territories, called redds. Aggression and display characterize many of the confrontations between the fish. Males bite, chase, and butt to ward off competitors. Females attack other females that appear to threaten their redd.

Garish coloration and grotesque distortions of jaws and teeth signal the onset of the adults' final days. This physical metamorphosis is caused by changes in fat composition, blood chemistry, hormones, enzymes, and skin pigmentation. Muscle softens and the skin thickens. White fungus may grow over sores or the eyes of the dying fish. The fins and tail fray from pounding against rocks. Wounds from predators or nets may mark the body. In spite of their rapidly deteriorating physical condition, the fish appear oblivious to pain and intent on one thing only: spawning.

FIGHTING MALES

THE FINAL ACT

Salmon spawning is a remarkable phenomenon to behold. Generally, spawning is broken into three types of behavior: redd selection and nest building, courtship and mating, and nest closure. Although individual species differ in certain behaviors, a generalized pattern occurs with all salmon.

Redd selection is the task of the female and is based on a variety of factors. Stream velocity, water depth, and gravel size determine the general suitability of a given site. The ability to claim and defend a redd site and the actual physical strength to excavate the nests vary with each fish.

Each species of salmon shows different preferences in terms of optimum spawning habitat. This ensures that available habitat is used efficiently with a minimum of competition. (For spawning habitat characteristics, see the Spawning Characteristics table on page 50.)

The redd is the general location selected by a female for laying eggs. Within that site, she may dig several nests and deposit eggs in them over a period of several days. The female begins by "nosing," an act in which she tests the gravel by probing,

FEMALE BUILDING A REDD

while cruising slowly over the bottom in the redd area. Having identified a suitable site, she turns on her side and begins flexing her body violently, slapping the gravel with her tail. This process dislodges gravel, which is lifted and carried slightly downstream by the current. After a series of digging motions, she swims forward and circles around to the downstream side of the nest to repeat the process. Sometimes the movements include tight circling or swimming over the nest in figure eights. Eventually, this produces a cone-shaped hollow varying in depth from just a few to as much as 15 inches (38 cm), depending on gravel composition and fish species.

The act of digging attracts males, who compete for the privilege of courtship. As a male manages to successfully ward off competitors, he joins the female in the nest in a series of movements that lead to egg and sperm release. The first of these movements is a "quiver," in which the male moves alongside the female and his body undulates slightly. He may follow this by "crossing over" the female near the base of her tail. As the nest develops, the female begins "probing" the gravel with her tail. Gradually, the probing increases and the circling decreases. The female

LAYING AND FERTILIZING EGGS

settles lower in the nest for longer periods. As this occurs, the male continues to quiver and frequently opens his mouth in a "gape."

As the female nears egg deposition, she begins to "crouch," a position much like the probe but with mouth agape. By opening her mouth, she increases her resistance to the current, which forces her deeper into the nest cavity. When the female assumes the crouch, the male quickly moves alongside. Both rapidly vibrate their tails and the eggs and sperm are released. The eggs emerge from the female one or two at a time into water clouded by the sperm, or milt. As this occurs, other males stationed outside of the nest may rush in to try to fertilize the eggs themselves. If the dominant male makes chase, another male may try to occupy the nest.

Early in spawning, as many as 1,200 eggs may be released into the nest, the number decreasing in subsequent nests. As they are released, current eddies in the depression pull most eggs downward into the nest to less turbulent water where sperm has settled and where they become lodged in the gravel.

As soon as the female has released her eggs, she instinctively covers them by moving upstream slightly and repeating her digging motions. This lifts gravel just above the nest, so that the current carries it into the depression. These "covering digs" in-

FEMALE COVERING EGGS

crease in intensity until the nest has been filled. Often the males will leave the female, in search of another that is preparing a nest. The female moves upstream slightly and begins digging a new nest. Spawning can last for several days. Once the females have deposited their eggs, they defend their redds until they die, about a week later. Males remain sexually active longer, roaming the stream in search of late females.

Gradually, the scene turns from a frenzied expression of life to a pathetic scene of death. Carcasses beach on the gravel, line the bottom, float downstream, and hang up in roots and limbs. Survivors swim listlessly, often drifting with the current. The scavengers arrive—ravens, crows, eagles, gulls, bears, and others. Footprints appear in the river sand overnight. The smell of rotting flesh rises out of logjams.

As the drama of spawning quiets with the death of the adult fish, the patient observer of salmon can take heart in what the process has yielded. The littered bodies, dragged into the shrubs and partly eaten, feed the entire forest. And underneath those fresh mounds of gravel on the stream bottom, thousands of eggs are already growing. The salmon are very much alive.

Spawning Behavior: A Guide to Watching

Observing wild salmon in the act of spawning requires a great deal of local knowledge, impeccable timing, and patience. It is much like birding: with a little practice, you develop the knack of anticipating where fish might be and refine your ability to identify species and understand behaviors that you see.

For surveying streams, important tools include polarized sunglasses, hip or chest waders, and a wading staff. You may want to bring binoculars for spotting from a distance or for watching other watchers, such as eagles and bears. If you know where spawning grounds are located and you can travel overland to the stream, wading may not be necessary. (Waders do run the risk of destroying eggs.)

Local knowledge comes from a variety of sources. You may already be a regular observer of the stream. You can also contact

fisheries biologists with state or provincial fish and wildlife agencies or local officials whose responsibilities include monitoring water quality or habitat resources. You can consult a local fishing supply store—once the "fish are in the creek," word travels fast among anglers. As spawning time approaches, visit the stream frequently, particularly after rainstorms, when water flows have increased. Identify places where you think fish might spawn; these include gravel banks with a brisk flow of water running over them. Look for logjams, cut banks, and deep pools, places where the fish may pause on their upstream journey. Fish are much easier to see if they are not moving. If there are barriers, like heavy rapids, falls, or culverts, develop the habit of surveying the pools just downstream.

Check for increased activity of predators. Gulls, eagles, and crows intensify their scavenging activities when salmon are in the creek; look for them perched in the trees above the water. Be on the lookout for other fish—cutthroat trout, for example, often follow the salmon right onto the spawning beds, where they feed opportunistically on eggs that are dislodged from the redds. Look also for that most significant of all predators, the angler. Finally, one very good clue you can detect from the road is a fish and wildlife agency vehicle parked near a bridge or boat ramp. Chances are that fisheries technicians are afield, conducting stream surveys or redd counts.

A sense of timing comes with local knowledge. Different stocks will spawn at different times. Knowing which spawns when will help you understand the fit of the fish to the local spawning habitat. In streams with chums and coho, the chums will often precede the coho and spawn lower in the system. The procession of stocks through a given area can last for several months.

Time of day can be important too, from the standpoint of available light and avoiding the glare of the overhead sun. Mornings and afternoons, when the shadows are long and angular, can be

SPAWNING CHARACTERISTICS

	Water velocity	Water depth	Bottom material	Avg. redd size	Avg. # of eggs	Egg depth
Chinook	high	11"–15"	coarse gravel and cobble	43–162 sq. ft.	3,000–7,000	7½"
Coho	highly variable	1½"–12"	silt to coarse gravel	30 sq. ft.	1,900–5,000	7"–15"
Sockeye	calm to moderate	3"–12"	coarse sand to cobble	approx. 34" × 40"*	2,800–4,000	6"–9"
Pink	brisk	12"–39"	gravel, sand mix	112 sq. ft.	1,200–1,900	avg. 7"–12"
Chum	moderate	5"–19"	gravel mixed w/ sand	29 sq. ft.	2,100–3,600	avg. 8½"
Steelhead	moderate	—	½"–3" gravel	70 sq. ft.	avg. 3,500	2"–12"
Cutthroat	riffle	7"	¼"–1" gravel	3 sq. ft.	300–2,700	7"

*single "nest" only

Sources: Groot & Margolis, Wydoski & Whitney

best for seeing deep into pools. Cloudy days can be either an advantage or a disadvantage: when there is no shade, even lighting can mean an even glare; on the other hand, darker skies can make viewing easier.

Cues to the movement of fish are important. Chinook and coho may breach in the river, betraying their movement by rolling or jumping on the surface. Large groups of fish can actually create wakes as they move through quiet waters. Approach a pool in the shadows, if possible, and give your eyes time to adjust to the darkness of the water.

Once the fish are on the spawning beds, they may seem oblivious to your presence. Avoid disturbing them, however—every bit of energy is critical to survival and spawning. Where you can, stay back from the stream, observing from the shrubs or other cover. Watch for as long as possible, so that you can see a variety of spawning behaviors. Then, if at all possible, return to the site several days in a row, so you can observe the whole progression of spawning.

The Endangered Wild Salmon

This book has focused on habitat as the key to salmon evolution, diversity, and health. Pacific salmon, particularly those of California, Oregon, Idaho, Washington, and parts of British Columbia, are under great environmental stress from habitat loss. Vast areas that once supported anadromous runs are now devoid of the fish because of dams that prevent access to historic spawning areas. Many unique genetic stocks have been lost—forever. Small streams, producers of many salmon, have been damaged by logging, filling, and pollution. Their stocks have been lost, or hover at dangerously low levels in many areas. Estuaries, the nurseries of young salmon, have been filled, dredged, or polluted. In some places, shorelines have been modified by the creation of bulkheads, eliminating the shallows that schools of juvenile fish seek for protection from large predators. In all, whole watersheds have been changed, one piece at a time, in ways harmful to salmon.

Another factor affecting the vitality of our wild fish has been the massive substitution of hatchery-raised fish for wild fish in many areas. The original tapestry of fish that evolved on our landscape has been "mended" with a mismatch of patches, in the form of fish well suited to handling, fast growth, and ease of production. What these fish lack, however, is the array of genetic material that would enable them to survive without the continued intervention of hatchery systems. What is most alarming is the lack of foresight on the part of fishery managers in assuming control over evolutionary processes that nature alone perfected over the millennia. The pressure to produce fish for commercial and sport fishers by focusing on quantity rather than quality has left a tragic genetic legacy.

The successful production of hatchery stocks has also harmed wild fish by fostering the belief that harvests will increase as hatchery populations increase. Because stocks mix when they are at sea, heavy harvesting actually *depletes* the weaker stocks.

But not all the news about salmon is negative; there are success stories too. Interested elementary and high school students have successfully restored spawning habitat and reared fish for reintroduction. Sport-fishing groups have raised money and volunteered to improve habitat and assist in the restoration of native wild stocks. State, federal, and tribal agencies have stepped up their research and management activities to learn more about and protect weakened stocks. And local governments have adopted stricter habitat protection laws through land-use and water-quality ordinances. Many other organizations have also become involved in monitoring and restoring fish habitat and wild populations.

If we are to save wild stocks of Pacific salmon, it will be by saving salmon habitat. We must first be able to know it when we see it and know how to protect it. We must learn that the watershed is the basic unit of habitat; anything that happens in the watershed has the potential to have a lasting effect on salmon. At the rates that our landscapes are changing—due to urban growth, logging, mining—our watersheds are being transformed. Streams that once flowed through cool forest glades now meander through open fields, clearcuts, or in culverts beneath blacktop. The absorptive power of the land has been reduced with roofs, roads, and bare ground. Environmental shock absorbers like forests, wetlands, and river floodplains have been lost. All of these factors have reduced habitat.

But the things that destroy salmon habitat don't all happen at the creek. Our kitchen sink is as much a part of the watershed as a forested (or logged) slope. Our dripping crankcase is part of the watershed. The storm drain on a street corner is part of the watershed; so is our lawn, septic drainfield, pasture, or feedlot. So is the parking lot at the office park or shopping mall. Even antifreeze and herbicide become parts of the watershed once they are out of their containers.

Improving salmon habitat begins with knowing that you are part of it and that your personal choices and actions can harm or protect it. The next step is to see salmon in that habitat and understand what is at stake. From there, many avenues for action are available. Start a personal journal; report comings and goings in your letters or conversations with friends; join an organization dedicated to habitat protection; participate in stream walks or cleanups or household hazardous-waste pickup days; volunteer at a school where kids rear salmon; plant seedlings along a creek; join a group that monitors water quality. There are many other possibilities!

Each of us, as individuals, can find many ways to protect salmon habitat. It begins within our homes, in our neighborhoods and our watersheds. Over time, the cycles of salmon, their comings and goings, can become important measures of the seasons. Most important, healthy local runs of salmon can signify the commitment of an entire community to its environment—a sign of environmental health we can all be proud to share.

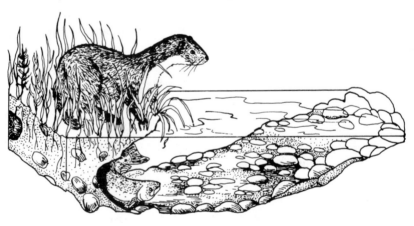

SALMON RANGE IN THE NORTHEAST PACIFIC

Chukchi Sea

Beaufort Sea

Colville R.

ALASKA

Noatak R.

McKenzie R.

YUKON
TERRITORY

Yukon R.

Sustina R.

Kuskokwin R.

Bristol
Bay

Gulf of Alaska

Skeena R.

BC

PACIFIC OCEAN

Fraser R.

WA

Columbia R.

OR

ALEUTIAN ISLANDS

Sacramento R.

CA

Salmon Sites

ALASKA

1. SHIP CREEK (ANCHORAGE) Kings (June), Silvers (August)
   The only *urban* fishing area in Alaska; fish ladder.

2. POTTER MARSH/POTTER CREEK/RABBIT CREEK
   (ANCHORAGE) Kings (June), Silvers (August)
   No fishing; good birding; fish are visible from a 1½-mile-
   long (2.4 km) boardwalk.

3. BODENBERG CREEK (PALMER) Reds (Sockeye) (July)
   On the old Palmer Alternate Highway; very close to the
   road; no fishing.

4. WILLIWAW CREEK (PORTAGE) Pinks (July), Silvers
   (August)
   Managed by the USFS; boardwalks; very popular; no
   fishing.

5. MENDENHALL GLACIER/STEEP CREEK (JUNEAU)
   Reds (late July to August), Coho (mid-August to October),
   Pinks (June to July), Chum (June to July)
   Visitor center.

6. LUNCH CREEK IN SETTLER'S COVE STATE PARK
   (KETCHIKAN) Coho (August to September)
   Where salt water meets fresh, 17 miles (27.2 km) north
   of Ketchikan.

7. WARD CREEK (KETCHIKAN) Coho (August to September), Pinks (July to September), Chum (August), Sockeye
   (July to September), Steelhead (April to May and November
   to December)
   Both above and below Ward Lake.

8. CHENA RIVER (FAIRBANKS) Kings (mid-July to mid-August), Chum (mid-July to mid-August)
Between the 39 and 50 milepost markers on Chena Hot Springs Road, especially at mile marker 46 (close to road); may require some walking.

9. DELTA JUNCTION Chum (mid-October to late November)
Huge runs; when Delta River freezes, chum gather at the springs, also bald eagles; short walk.

10. DELTA CLEARWATER RIVER Silvers (mid-October to mid-November)
Jack Warren Road; biggest silver spawning area in the Yukon drainage; 13 miles (20.8 km) north of Delta.

11. GULKANA RIVER Reds (late July)
Between Paxton and Summit lakes; interpretive signs on a very short walk from the road.

12. YUKON SYSTEM / BIG SALMON RIVER Kings (August)
Near Whitehorse; longest salmon migration in the world.

BRITISH COLUMBIA

13. ADAMS RIVER (KAMLOOPS) Sockeye (October)
World-famous sockeye run, as many as 1 million to 3 million fish; peaks every 4 years (1994, 1998).

14. COQUIHALLA RIVER (HOPE) Summer Steelhead (July)
At Tunnels Provincial Park; mostly wild fish leaping over obstructions in the river.

15. TRIBUTARY STREAMS TO KAKAWA LAKE (HOPE)
Kokanee (October)
Visitors should respect private property rights.

WASHINGTON

16. CEDAR RIVER — TRIBUTARY TO LAKE WASHINGTON (SEATTLE) Sockeye (late September to November), Chinook (late September to November)
Best viewing early October; area extends from Maplewood Golf Course upstream.

17. UPPER NORTH FORK STILLAGUAMISH Pinks (October)
Visitors should respect private property rights.

18. SKAGIT (ABOVE MOUTH OF THE SAUK RIVER) Pinks (October), Chinook (October)
Visitors should respect private property rights.

19. HAMMA HAMMA RIVER Fall chum (early December)
Visitors should respect private property rights.

20. DOSEWALLIPS RIVER Summer chum (early October)
Visitors should respect private property rights.

21. DUCKABUSH RIVER Pinks (October)
Only available in odd-numbered years.

22. MCALLISTER SPRINGS/NISQUALLY RIVER Winter chum (December to January)
City of Olympia water source.

23. SATSOP — TRIBUTARY OF CHEHALIS RIVER (MONTE-SANO) Coho (November), Chum (November)
East fork of the Satsop, near Schaefer State Park.

24. NORTH END LAKE LENORE Lahonten Cutthroat (April 1 to 24)
Very large cutthroat; just north of Soap Lake.

IDAHO

25. STOLLE MEADOWS/SOUTH FORK SALMON RIVER
Chinook (mid-August to mid-September)
At Warm Lake, 20 miles (32 km) from Cascade; boardwalk,
interpretive signs; mix of wild and hatchery fish.

26. RED RIVER — TRIBUTARY OF CLEARWATER RIVER
Chinook (mid-August to mid-September)
Interpretive information; developed by the Idaho Department of Fish and Game and the USFS.

OREGON

27. SANDY RIVER (PORTLAND) Fall Chinook (October)
Oxbow County Park.

28. STILL CREEK — TRIBUTARY OF THE SANDY
RIVER Spring Chinook (September to October)
Bridges provide access around private property.

29. MIAMI RIVER (TILLAMOOK) Chum (November)
Lower reaches, near Garibaldi.

30. SALMONBERRY RIVER Winter Steelhead (April)
13 miles (20.8 km) on Lower Nehalem Road from Elsie;
park at the mouth of the river and walk as far as 18 miles
(28.8 km) upstream.

31. PRINGLE CREEK (SALEM) Fall Chinook (September to
October)
Off Pringle Parkway in Pringle Park.
Mill Creek near the junction of Airport Road and State
Street (across from the Oregon State Penitentiary).
Mill Creek near the State Archives Building, south of the
state capitol.

32. LAKE CREEK FALLS FISH LADDER (EUGENE) Steelhead (February to March)
Near Blachly-Lane Campground, west of Eugene on Highway 36.

33. SHERAR'S FALLS/DESCHUTES RIVER Spring Chinook (April to early June), Fall Chinook (August to mid-October), Steelhead (August to mid-October)
Traditional Native American dip-netting; 8 miles (12.8 km) northeast of Maupin.

CALIFORNIA

34. FEATHER RIVER (OROVILLE) Chinook (October)

35. RED BLUFF DIVERSION DAM ON SACRAMENTO RIVER Chinook (October to November)
Salmon-viewing plaza.

36. TRINITY RIVER (LEWISTON) Chinook (mid-September to November)

37. SMITH RIVER SYSTEM Very clear river, excellent snorkeling; not great for fishing.

PATRICK CREEK (MIDDLE FORK) Chinook (early November to mid-January)
Easy access on Patrick Creek Road, ¼ mile (.4 km) above Patrick Creek Lodge; spawning structures (rock weirs) upstream; many other locations upstream are visible from pullouts on the road.

NILES CHRISTENSEN BRIDGE (SLANT BRIDGE) Chinook (early November to mid-January), Winter Steelhead (mid-January to April)
Junction of South Fork and Middle Fork; over a deep gorge.

RATTLESNAKE SLIDE (SOUTH FORK) Chinook (early November to mid-January), Winter Steelhead (mid-January to April) 2 to 13 miles (19.2 to 20.8 km) upstream from Niles Christensen Bridge, in the tail of Paradise Hole; observe from high points.

STEVENS BRIDGE Chinook (early November to mid-January), Winter Steelhead (mid-January to April) View pools downstream from the bridge.

G-O BRIDGE (SOUTH FORK) Chinook (early November to mid-January), Summer Steelhead (June to October) 1 mile (1.6 km) upstream from Stevens Bridge at the intersection of South Fork Road and G-O Road; view downstream from the G-O Bridge.

NORTH FORK Chinook (early November to mid-January), Winter Steelhead (mid-January to April)

To Learn More About Salmon

BOOKS

Brown, Bruce, *Mountain in the Clouds: A Search for the Wild Salmon* (New York: Simon and Schuster, 1982)

Childerhose, R. J., and Marj Trim, *Pacific Salmon* (Seattle: Douglas & McIntyre and University of Washington Press, 1979)

Groot, C., and L. Margolis, eds, *Pacific Salmon Life Histories* (Vancouver, BC: University of British Columbia Press, 1991)

Hart, J. L., *Pacific Fishes of Canada* (Ottawa: Fisheries Research Board of Canada, 1973)

Willers, W. B., *Trout Biology: An Angler's Guide* (Madison: University of Wisconsin Press, 1981)

Wydoski, Richard S., and Richard R. Whitney, *Inland Fishes of Washington* (Seattle: University of Washington Press, 1979)

Yates, Steve, *Adopting a Stream: A Northwest Handbook*, illustrated by Sandra Noel (Seattle: Adopt-A-Stream Foundation and University of Washington Press, 1988)

STATE/PROVINCIAL AGENCIES

Alaska Department of Fish and Game
P.O. Box 25526
Juneau, AK 99802-5526

British Columbia Ministry of the Environment — Fisheries
  Branch
780 Blanshard Street
Victoria, BC V8V 1X5

California Department of Fish and Game
1416 Ninth Street
Sacramento, CA 95814

Idaho Department of Fish and Game
600 South Walnut, Box 25
Boise, ID 83707

Oregon Department of Fish and Wildlife
P.O. Box 59
Portland, OR 97207

Washington Department of Fisheries
Room 115 General Administration Building
Olympia, WA 98504

Washington Department of Wildlife
600 Capitol Way N.
Olympia, WA 98501